For the Love
of Black Men

Books by Ayin M. Adams

Good Orderly Direction

For Ladies Only, Dedicated to the Color Pink

Kwanzaa in Hawai`i

African Americans In Hawai`i: A Search For Identity

The Woods Deep Inside Me

Walking In Sappho's Garden

Walking Through My Fire

Books edited by Ayin M. Adams

Climbing A Rainbow of Dreams

Butterflies Blossom

From Dawn To Dusk

Graffiti Dreams

For the Love of Black Men

Poems on Change, Life, Truth, and Trust

Ayin M. Adams

DELANE
PUBLISHING

ISBN 10
0990613917

ISBN 13
978-0-9906139-1-6

First Edition: April 17, 2015

Author's Photo by Ayin M. Adams
Cover Design and Typesetting by Saforabu Graphix
Front cover photos: © Photoeuphoria | Dreamstime.com
© Nilsz | Dreamstime.com
Back cover photos courtesy of abcnews.com and alan.com
Illustrations by Stacy Comer

Published by Delane Publishing
P.O. Box 195, Wailuku, Maui, HI 96793 USA
Email: books@delanepublishing.com
www.delanepublishing.com

Published in the United States of America

Printed in USA

Dedication

To all the black boys and black men
and their ancestors who persevered.

Contents

Foreword

For the Love of Black Men is a triumph for Ayin Adams' imaginative power – with poems reflecting the rich traditions and complexity of today's black society. Her new book awakens us to a black man's world in today's American Society with searing poems that stretch from the street to the healing power of family and love.

As a student of history and poetry since the 1960's, I've learned the best way to get rid of hatred is to get rid of secrets. From the chilling immediacy of *I Can't Breathe (for Eric Garner)* to the horrific truth of *Unarmed*, Adams tells apocalyptic moments in the Black community. But fear not, this poet, with *Return Home* and *A Special Feeling*, also encompasses the love, compassion and humor that connects the black man to the black community and to the world.

Fortunately for all of us, her verses actually become a legitimate shelf reference of America's shameful history of the slayings of unarmed black men. Reading her work is enough for me to urge you to share this book of poems with those you know and love.

Poetry reaching universal experience is fundamental to understanding human life and Adams connects the individual and the larger society – her poetry is Self meeting Self.

I believe poetry such as this belongs on every bookshelf to preserve contemporary history and to promote a greater truth for this nation. I'm delighted *For the Love of Black Men* is now available to everyone – of course, it makes me anxious too, will there be enough books for everyone to have a copy? So we can all read and then breathe the greater Air of Liberty?

Melinda Gohn; Coordinator for International Peace Poem Project
Hawaii Dr. Martin Luther King Jr. Peace Poetry Contest

Acknowledgements

I'd like to thank my father and my four brothers for their presence in my life. I like to thank my uncles and my four male cousins who escorted me home when they knew that it was too late for me to be out in the streets. Thank you to Gwyn Gorg, Stacy Comer, Linn Conyers and Mary Spratley who believed in me. Thank you to my sisters for their love and support. I like to thank the strong black mothers who held it together in the face of repeated bigotry and the death of their black sons. I'd like to thank my nephew Alquan who is an honest black man and a father. Thank you Universal Intelligence.

Introduction

For the Love of Black Men is a thought-provoking, hard-hitting book of poetry that offers renderings of past and present indignities, self-introspection, spiritual commitment, forgiveness and the necessity of solutions. It probes areas that are not openly discussed. More than just a book of poetry Ayin Adams' volume addresses issues credibly, compassionately, and directly, with a minimum of soft edges.

Adams transports the reader on a personal and private tour into a realm where some Black Men have had to wrestle and confront their own challenging questions concerning their wholeness.

> *A Portrait of Sadness*
> *A bruised heart with broken wings*
> *unable to take flight*
> *in the white winds of darkness.*

Many of the concerns these men have had to face may be similar to all men. However, because of the legacy of slavery, their obstacles are more. Black Male genitalia are generally believed to be larger than those of other races, but the legacy of slavery and poverty has produced insecure males whose penises can represent a false sense of power. The notion of a foot-long penis has incited fear in racists for generations toward a common goal of destruction by a hang- man's noose, a Billy Club, a choke-hold, a bullet or some other illegally immoral action. Adams writes in, *The White Woman and the Black Dick*

> *For years white men had tried unsuccessfully*
> *to protect their white women from the black dick*
> *in vain they try to protect snow white*
> *from his huge black bone crushing shaft.*

Experiencing the depth of rejection, where Black Men have been targets in need of strength, courage, forgiveness and education in order to survive has at times left a vacuum. Perhaps this void appears infinite, leaving nothing to grasp, except that tool which has been edified. In, *Numbing The Pain Through Sex,* Adams writes:

> *I shot my liquid rage into her and she believed*
> *I used manipulation and control for sex as power*
> *Knowing all the time that underneath it all*
> *was my own pain.*

The wholeness that is being sought is always present, even in the most desolate of times. Trusting one's inner source sometimes gives clarification to dilemmas that appear inconceivable. Many times silence or solitude are means by which answers are revealed. The fast-paced survival atmosphere in which most Black Men live does not provide such opportunities. In communities where there is a predominance of Black Men, the constant din of helicopters, fire-engines, sirens and other disturbances does not grant much contemplative time. An excerpt from the poem, *Father to Son,* Adams offers hope and the possibility of alternate choices.

> *From the auction block to the NFL combine,*
> *From Park Row to*
> *Park Avenue to Park Bench*
> *From building the White House to living in*
> *the White House as president of the United States.*

Ayin Adams' poetry addresses the Black Man from a potpourri of issues. A gentle and compassionate rumination shared in the loving description of *The Eyes of Father* while the contrast of *Sometimes I Feel Like A Fatherless Son* and the brutally truthful concerns addressed in *Hostage or Husband* offer objective assessments.

The single father, who brings his son to pot-luck social gatherings almost empty-handed, expecting a hand-out, is made to face his responsibilities in, *Save the Last Dance*

His face told the story of a beaten man
"You gotta contribute and not with snacks"
Hanging his head low nodding in agreement
he took off to the store, asking me to watch his son
"I'll do better than watch him, I'll feed him
"come here boy," I said in my gangster mother voice,
"today is your lucky day."

Love, Collard Greens and Cornbread shares a lighter, more amiable rendition of a Black Man in a comfortable, less stressful environment. In the poem, *Shorty's Juke Joint in Grover*

Josephine looks at Willie
"Good Lord, have mercy," Josephine thought
that man is a hot lion and I feel like his wide
open den where he can roam free.

Flirtatious and sexy told from a woman's private observation, a secret domain in which she can prudently come out to play.

When more opportunities for relaxation from the day to day grind of missed opportunities, minimum wage and fear become less prevalent, the distrust, sadness and pain will be reduced. When the trust and love of oneself becomes paramount then more doorways will be opened; psychologically, and physically.

I sit in my hotel room in New York City
Looking at a picture of the black men
in my family. Soon they will be coming to
visit me and the front desk manager will
call me to verify if these black men are here
to visit me , rape me, or mug me. I will tell the hotel Desk Clerk
"Yes, Mr. Hotel Clerk, please send them right up
and by the way, set a table for eight, we will be dining in the hotel
restaurant tonight.

This selection from *Nephews and Cousins* details some of the humiliation Black Men have to struggle with. Many times when Black Men enter an establishment, the non-blacks who are present, bristle and allow fear to overcome their sensibility.

It is essential for each Black Man to genuinely love himself, not at the expense of others but an ego-less love. Loving oneself may at times mean being quiet and taking several breaths. A real man does not have anything to prove and, as a consequence, can exemplify maturity. An intelligent man will not permit fear and anger to override his inward power. Being quiet is not compromising one's identity, dignity, integrity, nor manhood. Being quiet at the right time will prove your smartness to yourself and might save your life from fear-filled legal gun holders.

Adams reminds Black Males how essential it is for them to love themselves. She elevates them in familiar vernacular of their day to day beauty in the poem, *Beautiful Black Man*

> *be-bopping,*
> *finger popping*
> *tongue wagging*
> *Beautiful Black Man*
> *Handsome Black Brotha*
> *I just wanna say*
> *You so fine.*

In more recent times, approximately fifty plus reported cases of unarmed black men have been murdered by policemen which is a continuation of the 1857 original statement concerning Dred Scott, "No rights which the white man was bound to respect." Eric Garner, Michael Brown, Trayvon Martin were some of the victims who have given their lives. The ultimate questions being, Why or What For? Is an unsolicited martyrdom the ultimate reward for a Black Man, the final recognition that one never could have achieved on minimum wage or selling individual cigarettes with a second-class citizen mentality? The answers are always within, and the way in which we confront them will determine our happiness or unhappiness. The truth is that there is nothing to understand that is not in our very nature from the beginning. The only trip worth taking is the one that leads you to where you already are. In *Confrontation*

> *When he looked into the mirror, he was finally able*
> *to embrace all his shadow selves and come to welcome*
> *with open arms the small boy, the adult male the grown man*
> *and know that he is at the beginning of his magnificence,*
> *his strength, his own awakening.*

An excerpt from Adams' poem, *Dear Mother Letter*, written expressing views from some of the victims, presenting forgiveness as a courageous teaching, contrary to the feelings of many who will not give up their pain and resentment.

Dear Mother Letter
Mother I speak directly to you in your dreams, in your prayers and in the faces of other Black Men. Please know that we have made contact. Realize that deep down in your soul, we have reached one another. Know that I love you always mother and that I forgive everyone and I ask you to forgive them too, for they know not what they do. I am free. I love you. Your Son, Sean Bell, Amadou Diallo, Rodney King, Trayvon Martin, Michael Brown, Eric Garner, Tamir Rice and others whose seats that we keep warm and their lights which burn as they make their way home.

For the Love of Black Men exposes readers to an expansive reassessment of some of the issues that have prevailed since slavery which have produced myriads of confusion. Dr. Adams permits readers, participants, victims and those who have a genuine desire to rectify the problems, the hope that the offerings she has presented will illicit questions and perhaps provide some solutions. This book must be in everyone's library.

Gwyn Gorg, author of *I am The Blues.*

For the Love
of Black Men

RACE AND RAGE

Father to Son

Well Son, I'll tell you
life for the black man
ain't been no bed of roses
there were thorns in the cotton
we picked from the fields
of sweltering injustice
digging deep into our flesh
piercing us hauntingly
were the wounds of searing servitude.

We were shocked by the line that divided
us from them… the separateness
they claimed that bound them
clinging to their inferiority thinking it
to be superiority.

"Whites Only" clearly differentiates
"Colored" drinking fountain signs
hung like 'strange fruit' on a rusty nail.

Son, I'll want you to know that there was a time
when black folks sat at the back of the bus
and white men sprayed water canons
from fire hoses and let loose
sick rabid dogs to bite them.

But all the time son, we're still getting back up
every time we were knocked down
we were inhaling and exhaling
trying to draw air, breath by breath
we pulled tightly in that intangible air
we are holding on son, holding on to our prayers
holding on to our God, singing chants and dancing

with ritual on the black earth.
Our red blood ran its course and spilt
into the decaying streets, dried up like a raisin in the sun.

But all the time, we are holding on, holding on to our Ancestors
holding on to our future generations, we are marching, we are
walking with our hands up in the air, fists clinched in a movement
of Black Power, a movement of solidarity and a movement of
anger, and power to the people, we're not going to take this shit
anymore.

We are shouting: No Justice, No Peace, we walk like Michael
Brown, Trayvon Martin, and Eric Garner and other innocent black
men whose seed lay dead in the empty dark streets.

Son, I'll tell you
life for the Black man ain't been no bed of roses
there were thorns in 'em, digging deep into our flesh
piercing us hauntingly were the wounds of searing servitude.

From the mass Trans Atlantic route
to the planes of America.
From Abraham Lincoln to the Civil Rights
from the auction block to the NFL combine
from Park Avenue to park bench to park row,
from building the White House to living in the White House
as President of the United States.

Son, let me tell you, Black men are rising up
becoming leaders like Dr. King, Marcus Garvey, and Malcolm X.

Son, we live in a world that is governed by racism.
Son, don't ya give up now 'cause you find it's kinda hard

walk with your head high son
walk with your hands in the air, your pants on your waist
stand tall, black, and proud son.

Remember who you are son, remember that all the melanin
that flows through your veins is powerfully liberating
and extremely intoxicating.

It cannot be extracted from you, not even in death Son,
not even through white women who are sent to your bed.

Listen to learn and learn to listen son
listen to the sound of whistling
and when you hear whistling, think of Emmitt Till and all
the other little black boys who were lynched--
--unjustified homicide.

You possess the key to your race. You possess the key to humanity.
You possess the key to all races. No man has melanin,
except the black man and woman, use it wisely.
Ancestors speak, they say the wisdom that you have will save all
races.

Black Strength

You are clean and refreshing
as fallen rain.
You are the alpha and the omega.
You are a newborn baby.
You are the human race.
You are the beginning
and you are the end.
You touch the beauty of love
and present the grace of humility
in steadfast dedication.
Faith is power Black man
exercise your truth
exhibit your strength.

Erosion of the Black Man

Erosion of the black man
isolated, insulated, alienated
earth's crust separating
from the womb of mother Africa.
Erosion of the black man

transported thousands of miles
across continents…
isolated, insulated, alienated.

Loneliness dogs him
estrangement seeks him,
behold… the awakening
frightening indeed.

Erosion of the black man
isolated, insulated, alienated
lost between the first 3 inches
beneath his brown soil
collapsing around him
caving within.

Erosion of the black man
isolated, insulated, alienated
worn away, torn away, gone away, gone awry
isolated, insulated, alienated.

Missing is his systems of community and connection,
that always fosters nourishing and nurturing!

Racism

Glances
Rejections
Isolation
Laws
Traditions
Words
Actions
Racism felt by the Black Man.

Transition and Death

Cousin Sharon and I
went to Kings County Morgue
to identify the corpse
of our beloved Henry
a callous and senseless murder.

Henry lay stiff on the cold metal slab
his young life cut short
never reaching beyond the age of thirty years.

Blood drained from his ashen corpse
cousin Sharon's face crumbles in pain
tears streamed down her once bubbly brown face
using heavy fists as weapons
she pounded the walls
as they shook under her blows
numbness came to claim me.
Our heads bent over his frozen body
stroking his wavy curly black hair
between my fingers and watching his curls
unfurl and curl again.

Window of his soul stares at me through closed lids
his innocence, his unknowingness or perhaps
his knowing held the karmic answers
to help heal the generations of our people
to help relinquish the anguish of our people
of our black men, our sons, and our
brothers, our cousins, our nephews.

I stood above my beloved
searching for a sign, looking for a clue
hoping to find his murderer's DNA

stuck under his finger nails.
I scanned his naked body
asking myself, "Did he fight off his killer,
did he die in vain, pain, or did he die in fear?"

I sighed, Cousin Sharon pleaded and bargained with God
taking a red flask from her handbag
she raised the bottle to her lips
in hopes that strong drink would provide solutions.

She took another swig
and cursed the God of her understanding,
crying and asking, "Why, Why, Why?"
she sunk to the floor
battered by the storms of death
ravaged by a senseless murder
of our black brother.
We, as black women
learn to grow through love
we learn to move forward in pain
in life through death and transitions
which makes us strong for our people.

Loss and Grief

Our losses feed us
in miraculous ways
a meal filled with promise
from the womb to the tomb
and back again.

A baffling perverted carnal
mesh binds us.
Like a chick in the egg
we're always on the verge
of a whole new world.
We must be hatched or go bad.

Unarmed

Wendell Allen–unarmed, Alonzo Ashley–unarmed,
Anthony Baez–unarmed, Richard Brown–unarmed,
Aaron Campbell–unarmed, Amadou Diallo–unarmed,
Patrick Dorismond–unarmed, A. Demetrius Dubose–unarmed,
Jonathan Ferrell–unarmed, Jonny Gammage–unarmed,
Oscar Grant–unarmed, Gary Hopkins–unarmed, Nathaniel Jones–
unarmed, Prince Jones–unarmed, Irvin Landrum Jr.–unarmed,
Anthony Dwaine Lee–unarmed, Tyron Lewis–unarmed,
Roger Owensby–unarmed, Christopher Ridley–unarmed,
Timothy Stansbury–unarmed, Timothy Thomas–unarmed,
Robert Tolan Jr.–unarmed, Cornel Young–unarmed,
Ousmane Zongo–unarmed, Eric Garner–unarmed, and
Michael Brown–unarmed, _____unarmed,
_____unarmed, you fill in the blanks with the next name
of a black man!

What do they all have in common? They were all unarmed and killed
because the white man said that the black man has:

"No rights which the white man was bound to respect"
1857, 1957, 1987 1997, 2000, 2007, 2010, 2012, 2014, 2015

Are we reliving Dred Scott over again? Supposed to be living in a
Free State, but the pain, again, never ends, and our black man pays
again and again!

Horrors of injustice as a constant reminder while the Supreme Court
states that, "Dred Scott had no right to sue, because the white man
said that the black man has, "No rights which the white man was
bound to respect."

Truck the Supreme Court and its racist remarks of injustice!

We know that another black funeral is a nightmarish reminder,
and that they'll never find 'em guilty or render a conviction!
Buck the Supreme Court!

White police officers are killing our black men then cop a
plea called, "Property Damage" that's right, you heard me,
white police officers are getting kick backs, filled with black
hate, charge the state, property damage for a black man
bleeding and dying on his uniform.

Amadou Diallo, fired upon forty-one times
Sean Bell, the fifty-shot wedding day massacre
Billey Joe Johnson, brain matter as evidence
in plain sight when his car was returned to his parents!

Because the white man says that the black man has:
No rights which the white man was bound to respect!

And your white courts free your white cops
who murder and spill non-threatening black blood
while your government reaches settlements
for monetary consolation prizes!
Neither justice nor the value of human life
must never ever be in a position to be bought or sold
like slaves just because the white man says that the black man has:
No rights which the white man was bound to respect!

We demand reparations
you who have raped and plundered Mother Africa, we demand decency
and fair play
or be annihilated at last in hell!

And you say, the black man has:

No rights which the white man was bound to respect!
No rights which the white man was bound to respect!

Products of Tragic Mystification: Homophobia

Products of tragic mystification
Homophobia
Products of tragic mystification
Homophobia, Homophobia, Homophobia
Rooted deep
Deep within his sexuality
Fosters insecurities
Insecurities and co-dependencies
Co-dependencies and using me
all are
Products of tragic mystification
Homophobia!
Mystification, mystification,
Mystified friendships
Products of tragic mystification
Homophobia!

Poem For a Gay Man

You both lay
on the white sands beaches of Maui
in the quietness of a starry night
as stars reveal the love
of your hearts aflutter.

Ocean breeze stir waves
that run on the shore and flow back to sea again.

Under the cover of a full moon
your black skin glistens and shimmers
like two coins thrown into the fountain
wishing for luck.

I breathe in your trust
and roll over in your waiting arms
oh lover, breathing in the quiet air
under the coconut trees
on the beaches of sweet Maui.

For Ross

Yes, I was angry with you
when you had sex
with nineteen year old Jason.
I told you to leave him alone
I remember telling him to leave you alone also.

Silly was I to think that two gay boys
would listen to one who lay between
the legs of bubbling brown sugar.

Now Jason cries with news of your status
wondering if he too will test positive
for HIV AIDS.

The hostel where you died,
they said you paid $30.00 for the night and
your spirit still haunts the place.

Post Racial Racism

Institutions
Convoluting
Processes
Confines
Procedures, seizures
Measures
Interactions
Galactic
Practices
Confines
Illuminate
Perpetuate
Copulate
Opiate
Confines.

The White Women and the Black Dick

For years white men had tried unsuccessfully
to protect their white women from the black dick.
In vain they try to protect snow white
from his huge black bone crushing shaft.

This sexual act between the two
considered immoral.
He, described as a fixed Black Devil.
She, as pure as the driven snow.
He, as depraved and abnormal whose meat
weighs 15 pounds.

Him, sold off the auction block
to procreate more black babies
to work slave master's fields, turfs, and courts
and sometimes the white cold slippery ice.

A thronging size
of misappropriation for the black man.
White women yell rape to lynch a black man,
now she craves and begs
for the cocked hammering sledge,
banging, thrusting, tearing, ripping
of black meat to strike her
between her weak white thighs.

Numbing the Pain through Sex

I was broken, empty, and unholy
principles seemed foreign.
I had no tools, except the one I used to trap her
bind her tight, with all my might
false as I was, she took the bite
in a world of humiliation, fear, and shame
a pretense world the same, with no change.
I used my gun as a weapon against her and myself.
I used my penis like a ruler to measure her pain,
I calculated her loneliness, subtracted her fear
then penetrated her, all the while hiding my own pain.
The more vulnerable she became, the more scam I put
into my game, her weakness fed my power, at any hour, my own
discontent... sent her... because she needed to feel wanted,
she needed to feel loved, she needed to belong, she needed a man
any man... and I needed to feel better about myself.
I scammed myself numbing the pain through sex
gyrating hips assaulted her, sweet surrender under manipulation
stimulation, undulation, and copulation.
She cried and I thrust harder. She lay hoping that we were building
a world together and I reaching for power outside myself.
Fighting back my own tears, my own shame, my own degradation
I sexed her into submission, I took her body.
I took her mind, and then I took her money.
I shot my liquid rage into her and she believed me.
I played her like a fiddle and used my control for sex as power
knowing all the time underneath it all was my own pain.
I was numbing my pain through sex.

Tick Tock Clock Stop

Tick
    Tock
        Tick
           Tock
The clock has stopped
all hands down
the well of grief
    the well of grief
        the well of grief.

We take our cue
from cold dead lips
in silence
a coffin
a hearse
the well of grief
    the well of grief
        the well of grief.

Eric Garner's Grave; Plot 8B Rosedale Cemetery, New Jersey

Just Do It

Statement of the Cause:
      Reparations take responsibility
    Guilt takes blame
Love takes courage.

Legacy of Slavery

The legacy of slavery
is about divide and conquer.

The black man will not
seek out a black sistah
or a black licensed Social Worker,
or a Ph.D. or a black therapist
for professional mental help.
The black man seeks out a white therapist.

The legacy of slavery
is about divide and conquer.

The white therapist does not
know the black man's struggle
does not know his hustle
and definitely does not know his concerns.

The white therapist knows "only"
The black man's place:

"Sit down, shut up, and just listen. I'll
tell you how to live your life."

He scratches his head and responds,
"Yesum."

A Vicious Cycle

Slavery is...
A vicious cycle

Crimes against humanity...
Slavery is...
A vicious cycle

Treated with particular cruelty during perpetration...
Slavery is...
A vicious cycle

Degree of physical harm...
A vicious cycle

Lynching...
A vicious cycle

Whippings...
A vicious cycle

Lashes...
A vicious cycle

Death...
A vicious cycle

Negative influence on history...
A vicious cycle

Slavery...
Is a repetitive pattern
A vicious cycle.

SEEDS

Barcelona Brownsville

Barcelona Brownsville
raised in the hood
shot at the po-po
from the roof of Howard Houses
sold weed and collected guns
by the numbers as a hobby.

One day he got a call
saying he was the father of a baby girl.
DNA test proved that he was indeed
the baby's father.

The game of life changed
for him the day he got the news
that he was a father.
He always said, that he would never
have any babies with "females"
as he called them. But Haven was different;
from the first time he held her tiny body
in his strong black arms, he grew into a man
and wore his badge proudly.

Haven became his light, his world.
Barcelona Brownsville raised his daughter
like a man is supposed to raise his child.
He read bed-time stories to Haven,
cooked lavished meals for her and even braided her hair.

Next he moved and bought Haven a two bedroom
townhouse to raise her. It was just the two of them
living happy, joyous, and free.

Barcelona Brownsville never needed the courts

to define his love for his daughter
nor his consistency at raising his child.

Yep, the day Haven came into his life,
Barcelona Brownsville's life changed for the better.

Child Support Payments and the Black Man

Baby's Momma
                 Petitioner
     vs.
Baby's Daddy
                 Respondent

REGISTRATION OF SUPPORT ORDER

The Child Support Enforcement Agency registers
with the Family Court of AnyWhere in the USA.
A registration statement, or a sworn statement or
certification of the amount of the arrearage, if any,
which we know there is. We are concerned
with the amount that has accrued during the
specified time period.

The Child Support Transmittal has been received
from any state in the USA requesting registration
of the child support order for the purposes specified
therein.

In compliance with the provision, black man, you
are hereby notified that petitioner or baby's momma
have taken you to court to get money from you to
take care of your baby. This constitutes notification
that your support order, is enforceable as of the date
of registration in the same manner as an order issued
by the Family Court, the Child Support Enforcement Agency,
or any other Tribunal of any state anywhere in the USA.

You are further notified that you may request a
hearing to contest the validity or enforcement of
the registered order. The request must be made within

seven days after the date of mailing or personal service of this notice. Failure to contest the validity of the order and the alleged money owed precludes further contest of the order with respect to any matter that could have been asserted.

Please read the sworn statement of the amount of the arrearage, that indicates that the amount owed is $14,400.00 and said arrearages accrued during the period(s) of three years 4/1/2012 to 4/1/2015, up until age 18 in the year 2030, child support shall be $72,000.00

The Child Support Transmittal that has been received is requesting registration of the child support order for the purpose specified therein. From this time forward, you are ordered to pay your support to:

Child Support Enforcement Agency
P.O. Box Tracking You Down
Pay Your Bills, Black Man, USA
13252-1234

The Child Support Enforcement Agency
shall then transmit said payments to:

Child Support Receipting
GBMC or Get Black Man's Check
Urban City, Anywhere USA
Ghetto, 12345

or such other agency or person that the
Child Support Enforcement Agency

deems appropriate to receive such payments.

The name and address of the oblige is as follows:

Baby's Momma
C/O Sperm Donor's Check
21 Black Jack Baby or
456 Cello Babyboy
Get Paid, USA 56789-1011

Seeds That Bind

He
dreamed of marriage
and fatherhood
His light flickered
Her wetness oozed
guiding him home.

She
opened wider
ready to receive him
tower of power in
seeds deeded by heritage

bearing their strong melanin
that solidified Truths
among all the races.

She knew that he found safety in her jewels
they smiled in unison, deeply he thrust
openly she received him,
as he returned home at last.
Rightful place for King and Queen
and their offspring.

Blues for the Black Man

I lit a candle for you today
no matter how far you run
no matter how long you avoid me
I lit a candle for you today.

Mother Maui is ever so small
yet gentle with healing in her sacredness
for you, so I lit a candle for you today.

I remember a moment in time
praying for you
"I am a grown ass man," you said
then stormed off with hands in pocket,
head bent, sucking your teeth
as a small boy might do when wrong.

Knowing that prayer heals discord
deep down in the scarred soul
I chastised your reactions to emotions that run astray
patted your frail shoulders and hugged you anyway.

I lit a candle for you
for the resurrection of your
hopes -dashed-
purification of your pain–burnt.

I tried to help tame you
calm you, your fears, your jeers and tears
unending questions you seek
of your place as a Black man
in this "unforgiving world" you cried.
I caught the torment in your eyes
hidden where your fire used to blaze bright.

Now dimly sparkle confusion
stares out the windows of your soul
pleading for you, to awaken from your long sleep.

I lit a candle for you today
to encourage your soul
to return home, return home
find peace at last black man, find peace.
I lit a candle for you today.

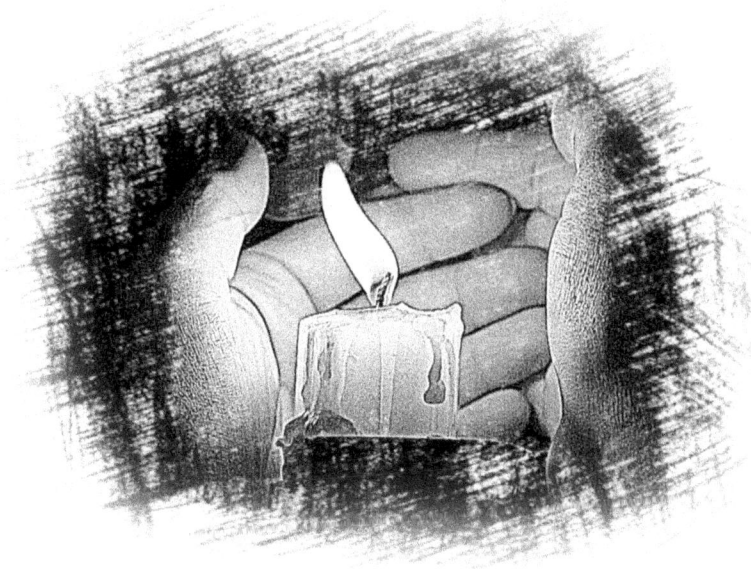

A Special Feeling

There is a special feeling that you get
when you see a black man dressed in a suit.

There is a greater feeling you get
when you see a black man wearing a tie
and he's standing tall and looking good.

There is a special feeling you get
when you see a black man
and he is walking down the street
in his uniform with his black sistah
walking hand in hand.

There is a special feeling you get
when you see a black man who sees himself
and he knows where he came from
where he has been and where he is going.

There is a special good, greater, omnipotent feeling
you get when you look into a black man's eyes
and see your son, your brother, your father, your male cousin
and the great One who birthed great black men
----------------------WOMAN----------------------

Watering Seeds

Some seeds are planted
some seeds are aborted
some seeds never take root
some seeds need watering
some seeds need care.

Between the sheets of last night romp
bitter feelings awaken, shaken confidence
stale wine and cigarette butts clogs the air
shoes in hand, he tip toes out the back door
never once looked back, never gazed back to see
his seed grow, develop, read, write, sustained,
nurtured, live, or die.

You never looked back to see if weeds were
strangling the baby seeds,
choking sacred life,
the very berry breath of
Black life that matters!

When will you rise up?
When will you sing your song?
When will you pay homage?

Who is that boy?
Where is that Black Man?
Speak up!

I am that boy, I am that black man
who will tend the brown dirt, fertilize the earth,
and bless the new born seeds.
I will announce publicly
we together will grow my child

and plow through the seasons
weather storms and know the reasons
why the caged bird now sings
and that I too am the darker brother
who sits in the kitchen when company comes.

My sons and my dykes, should they choose
to live a life of GLBT, together we will walk
in this world, together we will stand and plant
the first fruits.
We will rise and take control of our harvest.

His Soul Sings Acappella

He sits in silence, desiring not to interact
early morning showers captivates his ears
rain drizzles, mingles with reluctant tears.

Soft cries echo to whispering winds
majestic peaks of the West Side Maui mountains
casts a blanket shadow over his lean frame.

Iwa birds fly to nearby roof gutters
in hopes of escaping wet wings.
A lotus opens its petals to revitalizing love
he hopes of mirroring sacred serenity found within.

Petals bloom, iridescent and sweet
like delicate fragrances of Puakenikeni.

Fluttering butterflies sparkle like magic
overhead dark skies stare permanently
still.

His own life, his story, weaved and wovened
through melancholy emotions and upheavals.
The tapestry of years
the fabric of discontent and restlessness
embedded to the core, finally erupting, he now feels
the ending of this journey, already written and told
that she left by plane. Neighbors gossiped about
how she left him. True to the rivers of a wretched past
he now awakens to the reality of a new beginning.
His soul sings loud.
His soul sings with new meaning.
His soul sings acappella.

Nubian

Savage
Black
Brute
Big
Burly
Sexual
Heathen
N _ _ _ _ r

I know you want to call me
negative racial names
call me by our rightful name
Nubian!

Love

Love yourself Brotha
Love your life Brotha
Love your sistah Brotha
Love your peace Brotha
Love your rights Brotha
Love your Love Brotha
Love your cause Brotha
Love your honor Brotha
Love your mother Brotha
Love your black baby Brotha
Love your Brother, Brotha
Love Love Brotha
To love often
Love! Love! Love!

Tree of Life

You are a vitally needed
essential part of a system
that breathes and harnesses energy
deep in the depths of human earth.
To see you playing small
reminds me of your greatness
and how together we breathe
the oxygen of your essence.
You have transformed the elements
of your pain into rain, that cleanses and shines
light where there is darkness
and nourishment for your limbs and branches.
You are connected to all your people
from the bark and the root
through a healing, affirming
kaleidoscope of relationships.
We need each other to survive and thrive.

The Eyes of Father

I never saw hatred in the eyes of Father
though he could lock eyes deep and stare long
through his pretty brown eyes.

I never saw sadness in the eyes of Father
though he carried a heavy heart
and the fact that he was a black man
but he could laugh out loud
because he was gentle and caring.

I felt content in the arms of father
a special feeling he created
by making time to be with me
although we had a large family
who wanted time with him too.

The scars of his own life
scars of his difficult childhood
scars of his own three brothers' lives.

Scars of his life stored deep
buried, chained, padlocked, hidden,
forgotten and left unspoken.

Emotionally he carried heavy unwanted scars
but you could never tell
Father covered up deliberately and swapped hurt for joy
even when mother's father died.

Behind the eyes of father
I could feel shimmering smoldering
pockets of frustrations
strangled dreams that were unfulfilled

hopes lost in abandonment
too little money
humiliation, degradation, assimilation into culture
and isolation within father's self
unable to tend the fire of his soul
that burned with passionate desire
this made his brown eyes restless.

A restlessness that made him move the furniture
around the house every so often
as if it might impress visitors
as if it might look new.

It was hard on father,
but his heart made up for that.
He had a big enough heart
to share his food from his fields
with neighbors, community and friends.

Father did not try to belong to any class of people
not the poor, nor the middle-class bourgeoisie.

He was a sweet soul
who gave in to mother all the time
I defied him once when speaking my mind
a bitter taste left over in my mouth.

Nearing the end of his time
I paid him a visit
he wanted his hair combed and scalp scratched,
said it felt good

Precious time shared between us

telling stories about my birth
and why he never called me by my real name
and building the railroad tracks in the South with grandfather.

I gave him money which he eagerly took and smiled,
a wide grin revealing his white teeth with glee.

The candle will flicker in his eyes
and flicker on my altar
when he gives up his ghost
I will assist him on his journey
I will release tears from my eyes
and see into father's eyes and he will know
this will be the first time I will cry for Father.

Sometimes I Feel Like a Fatherless Son

There are times
there are moments
that I feel like a fatherless child
alone, cold, frightened, lost, and scared.

It is the hopeless feeling against all hope
it is the loveless activity that does not reach the heart
to heal the pain, or mend broken veins.

It is when tragedy strikes
not once, or twice, but three times
and there is no one who will protect me
against the eyes in shadows that prey and watch
no one to light the fire to keep me warm.

Shelter I seek is far, it is a distant memory
endless miles stretch against the road less traveled
grainy sand washes out to sea
with tides that hide in pools
behind the crevices of silence
and then is gone again
like two sheets in the wind
reflecting my own betrayals, wounds, hurts,
the curse and within it all is a seed,
a tiny mustard seed filled
with the faith of a small fragile and wanting child
that never gives up but seeks to love and to know
for a way opening up, his own inner imprisoned splendor!

Change Agents

1850-1860

Civil War
Racism
Pathology
White Supremacy

1960

Civil Rights
Dr. King, Malcolm X,
Stokley Carmichael
Angela Davis
Change Agents

2008-2016

Barack Hussein Obama
First Black Sitting President
United States of America
in White House.

A Grown Ass Man

A grown ass man
does not throw temper tantrums.
A grown ass man
does not suck his thumb
as if he were caught with
his prick in his hand.
A grown ass man
does not mope around the house.
A grown ass man
does not argue with his woman
whether she is right or wrong.
A grown ass man
does not disrespect his mother.

A grown ass man
is mature.
A grown ass man
is kind and gentle, and loving.
A grown ass man
owns his mistakes
and makes admission
for harm caused; real or imagined.
A grown ass man
will pick up the twenty pound telephone
to a squash a beef with any man or woman.
A grown ass man
will love hard on his black sistah.
A grown ass man
will provide for and protect his family,
his sistahs, and his house.
A grown ass man will love hard
and cry openly.
A grown ass man feels his pain

shows his pain, honors his growth
and recognizes his strength.
A grown ass man
will rise to live in harmony
with his world including nature.
A grown ass man is powerful
when he expresses his spirituality
and talk about the love of God.
A grown ass man realizes his maturity
and let petty peeves dissipate.
A grown ass man
accepts his premise,
his growth, and his unfolding good.
A grown ass man
knows his spiritual purpose
and accepts the premise that he is
to live life more abundantly.
A grown ass man
knows that if he does not desire to be
in a certain place, he will remove himself.
A grown ass man
knows that at the end of the day
he has got to make a decision
as a man, and he has got to live with his decision.
All these things, a grown ass man knows.

Secret Issues

He has no male friends
he has no black male friends
no one to drink a beer with
never wear shorts
no one to give objective feedback
fear of self
fear of wife
fear of life
filled with anger
filled with hate
that frustrates
there is no need to control another
deep down inside he cares
even if he is a light skinned brother
if he forgives
he will then grow up
and give up his fear
give up his hatred
and give up his secret issues.

RETURN HOME

Shorty's Juke Joint in Grover:
Josephine Looks at Willie

His light brown eyes and tight ass
with chocolate smooth bulging biceps
busting out from his unbuttoned short sleeved shirt
but it was his white pearly teeth and flashy smile

she fixated her eyes on him
like midnight stars and bright lights
on an MGM movie set.

Josephine looked at his feet to measure his Johnson
next she surveyed the slow grind of his hips
swaying and gyrating to the beat of the music.

She sucked in her gut, placed her hands over her heart
she wanted to sit down, but she was already sitting
with her thighs pressed tightly closed.

Willie threw his head back, sprayed the ceiling
with the joy of his laughter
precariously he did a little dip to the beat
of the undulating song
their eyes met momentarily
as he came up from the dip.

"Good Lord, have mercy," Josephine thought,
"that man is a hot lion and I feel like his wide
open den where he can roam free.

He Who Walks Tall

Strong black boy
He who walks tall
strong black boy
walking proud
African warrior
pillar of power
tower of strength
drummer, dancer
worshipper of Ancestors
sacred rituals
mystical man
controlling
flames of fire
passionate
your soul is.
Be the true magician.

Beautiful Black Man

Beautiful black man
handsome black brotha
I just wanna say
you so fine
with your long locks
short cropped, tank top
bald top
gliding down the street
be-bopping
finger popping
tongue wagging
whistling at me–Yeah!

Beautiful black man
handsome black brotha
I just wanna say
you so fine
your treasure is full of pleasure
crap games, week working,
rooftops, hallways,
pimping your ride
hollering at me.

Beautiful black man
handsome black brotha
I just wanna say
you so fine
wearing your Nike, Air Jordan,
Sean John, Fubu,
and that bulging spot
hot, yellow gold stain
pushing, rushing, blushing
seeking to escape.

I throttle, laugh, and scream,
holler, jump up and down
because you compliment
desires arising
fires to fan, flames to ignite
the soul of you.
Beautiful black man
recommends my soul
like no other black brotha!

Loving Him

Arms will hold you in love
unconditionally .
You have freedom
freedom from
freedom to
to be
to have
to hold
to grow
my love
always
bring you deep
within the wells
of safety
into the moist caves
of strength
allowing passion
to awaken
to
truth
of essence
Black Man
Black Woman.

Gratitude
(for Sugar)

I appreciate your listening skills.
I appreciate that you are supportive.
I appreciate that you are a fantastic lover
I appreciate that your laughter melts my sadness
I appreciate you cooking for me always.
I appreciate that you are easy, fun-loving, care-free spirit.
I appreciate your attention.
I love your strength.
I appreciate you.
I am grateful.

Love, Collard Greens, and Cornbread

She knew how to win her man over
she caught her man through food
she cooked her most prized possession
a famous recipe handed down from generations to generations
love, collard greens, and cornbread.

Sunday she served him collard greens, cornbread
and southern fried chicken
she topped it off with a pitcher full of
red Kool Aid.

He kicked his shoes off
laid down on the sofa
next to his sistah
relaxed in her love.
She knew she had won him
when his socks came off.
If a black man does not
take his socks off in your house
girlfriend, he is not staying!
Satisfying food fills his thirst
he spills his love into her warm springs
of becoming one.

Love, collard greens and cornbread
does a black man good.
He remembers when he was a small boy
with his mother and sisters in the kitchen
listening to their stories while waiting to grow up.
He too would want a black woman
who had those kitchen stories of his youth
to share, to laugh, to remember culture and
to keep his Ancestors alive through

their common thread of shared stories.
No other woman except the black woman
has these stories for the black man, and
with the black man and through the black
generations of love, cornbread, and collard greens.

Return Home

Return home
return home now
to the inner
sanctuary of black love.
Black woman's love
nestled in joy
laying between chocolate thighs
take her, take self
merge together as one
in your sacred black journey!

Nephews and Cousins

I sit in my hotel room in New York City
looking at a picture of the black men
in my family. Soon they will be coming to
visit me shortly and the front desk manager will
call me to verify if these black men are here
to visit me, rape me, or mug me. I will tell the hotel
desk clerk that:

These handsome young tall black men
are my family, they are beautiful strong men
I recall each of their births vividly
as I stood over them and prayed that
their little penises when adult size
would not hurt women.

Each diaper I changed, each bottle I fed them
in my arms, I sung lullabies into their DNA
to remember their power and the power of their black penis.
I cautioned my nephews and cousins to not squander their essence
but to always remember Emmett Till.
I sang sacred lineage songs given to me
by our ancestors to escape the lynchings.
I sang to their chariot hearts to bear witness to the chains of
generations they could break and did break to live past the ripe
old age of 18 which is considered an old timer if you live in the
Borough of Brooklyn.

"Yes, Mr. Hotel Clerk, please send them right up
and by the way, set a table for eight, we will be dining
in the hotel restaurant tonight."

Too Many Days

For too many days now
I have not seen the brown man walking
from Paia town towards Hana Highway.

For too many days now
I have not seen the seven foot white cross
that he carries five miles long
in the hot sun and five miles back to Paia town.

For too many days now
I have not seen his toothless grin smiling at me
nor motorists laughing at him in passing cars
as he faithfully communes his daily ritual.

For too many days now
I have not seen his blessed kisses
sprinkling me with glee as I pass him driving by.

For too many days now
I have not given myself over
to the God he daily cherishes
nor the depths of his commitments
to a practice of steady trust
nor love unconditionally
and pray for people in passing cars.

But now, I have spoken of this great charge
I have spoken of this great feat
this endeavor
the consistency of claiming a devoted practice
to which I too can belong
the currents of inner longings
and the shifting of high tides

stirs within me
between the channels of balance
I feel full and ready to take flight.

I am ready now. I am ready for that great claim
I am willing to claim all parts of myself
that longs to grow, that embraces my quiet strength
on a journey that lives deep inside me
that lives deep inside me, that lives deep… inside me.

Save the Last Dance

He never bought a pot-luck dish
to any black cultural event
other than a small box of animal crackers
for 39 cents and a bag of potato chips for 25 cents
for his black mixed son.

Folks numbered about 30
depending on him to bring food, the people
would surely starve and perish.
Everyone knew he didn't bring food
but no one questioned him or helped him
live to be better and braver
than his smallness allowed.

He would walk over to the food table
drop the box of crackers and chips on the table
trying to fake others out.
I always watched him because I knew he was a dead-beat
freeloading bum-ass punk standing over the table,
suggesting that he contributed.

Pretending to stand by the table surveying
bountiful food dishes that other folks had
bought that would fill his son's empty belly
as well as his belly too.
It wouldn't be so bad, if he'd only bought enough
to feed the others and spent $15.00-$20.00
on something hearty and meaty too.

I watched every time we met.
His son would arrive hungry, because he did not eat breakfast.
His son was confused and didn't know much about black folks
and didn't show any traits of wanting to learn.

"Papa, I'm hungry" the starving boy whined.
Ignoring the stabbing pains in his son's belly,
he'd been there for only five minutes
and it was considered "bad taste" to eat immediately upon arrival.

"Wait, boy, wait," he would sheepishly echo to his hungry son.
The boy snatched the animal crackers off the table and
ran towards the ocean to eat them safely away from prying eyes.

A few minutes later, the boy would return
to the table again hungry still.
Others watched, said nothing,
I, observed all this, then stepped to the brother
in my own cocky don't give-a-damn-attitude-
from the streets of Brooklyn and said,

"Listen here brother man, you need to go
across the street to the supermarket
bring some chicken and bread back
that all of us can eat."

His face told the story of a beaten man. I said to him,
"You gotta contribute and not with snacks"
hanging his head low nodding in agreement,
he took off to the store, asking me to watch his son.
"I'll do better than watch him, I'll feed him."
"Come here boy, "I said in my gangster mother voice,
"today is your lucky day."

Our Eyes Meet

Iao was quiet today
I laid down near her body
barely hearing her soft murmur.
Waves trickling, touched my naked body
tender caress as a gentle lover
even the birds stopped chatting
through mango trees
just to see our eyes meet.
Iao dances upon slow
moving streams.

As fallen stars burst, closing my eyes, I felt you
black beauty, curling up in the spoon position
lolling over, our eyes meet,
lock, holding a precious loving stare
reflecting in the mirror of water
the true face, the true face of our own.

I taste your succulent lips beloved
sweet delight, your honey tongue
sticks to my heart, warms my belly
feed naughty thoughts to my mind
smiles erupts
for one magic moment
I fell the ballad of Silent Iao
as we embrace
rainbow lovers
Black beauty
strong, masculine
balanced.

Facts

Four things must be recognized:

- All men are created equal
- Slavery happened to Black People
- Get it Right
- Take Responsibility

One thing to do:
- Repair the damage that was done!

Healing

In order to heal we must talk about the past
we must be willing to talk about what is wrong.
In order to heal we must look at patterns
we must be willing to look at moral issues.

In order to heal we need to be heard
you must be willing to listen to our story.

In order to heal you must know
that those who hate Blacks
hate with a conviction.

In order to heal you must love.
We must love those who hate
and those who hate us with a conviction.

In order to heal
human suffering must be removed.
You must be willing to see blacks
at a juncture reaching critical mass.

In order to heal
you must take responsibility.
You must be truthful enough
to know that reparations takes responsibility
and guilt takes blame.

In order to heal you must know
what you have done and be willing
to repair the damage that was done
even by your father's father's father's father.
Healing, healing, healing, and healing!

Freedom Matters

There is a negative peace
and there is a positive peace.

We want to be heard
we have a story.

There is a negative peace
and there is a positive peace.

We stand on an idea:
Cultural Freedom

What do you stand on?
What is your story?

Loosies

Loosies were sold on my block back in the day
and the cops never said anything or did anything.
Store owners would open up a pack of cigarettes;
and hide them near the cash register
out of the prying eyes of adults.

The Arabs and Puerto Rican Bodega store owners
were illegal aliens who stole away from their country
into Ellis Island, New York City for a better life.

We used to walk to the corner store to buy our smokes;
two loosies for a nickel. We were teenagers, cool and
with no worries. We would put one loosie behind our ear
and the other loosie between our fingers, puffing and
bopping down the street. We were cool kids
who smoked Newports or Kool menthol cigarettes.

Years later, one loosie cost a dime, then two loosies
cost a quarter, now today, one loosie goes
for fifty cents. There was never any cops detaining,
arresting, or killing a black men for selling a loosie.

Whatever happened to the good ole' days of the beat street cop
who took on 20 criminals, whistled Dixie, sang to the sun
while Momma poured him a glass of ice tea from her porch?

This is not a good time to be living as a black man in 2015.

For the Love of Black Men

To love the Black Man or to love any man is a spiritual
commitment. You must love yourself, know yourself,
and you must understand who you are loving.

Without knowing yourself, you can never know anyone else
much less know the black man, know his pain, or even know
his generational struggle.

You must know what it entails to commit to love
For the Love of Black Men, and you must know what love
suggests and you must know what love means
when the word growth is expressed.

Love is not defined by being in a relationship, nor is it defined by
going through a relationship, it is defined by growing through a
relationship that enhances and augments his and your personal
spiritual growth.

For the Love of Black Men seeks successful relationships
that includes healthy discussions and engenders mature
experiences being open and receptive as each one teaches one
while expressing wants, needs, dreams, ideas,
and respecting the unfolding process during difficult situations.

For the Love of Black Men embodies loving and caring
for our bodies and ourselves with an open heart.
For the Love of Black Men is the love we carry
as we remember our ancestors tarried respecting the truth
that all black lives matter.

A SEASON OF DISCONTENT

Bullets of Hate

Fall to the bullets of hate
in state, we lay on display
a small box contains the remains
sustains, jewels for viewing.

Fall to the bullets of hate
in state, we lay on display
a small box contains the remains
sustains, jewels for viewing.

We must cultivate compassion.
We must cultivate responsibility.
We must cultivate humility
and know that all lives matter.

Fall to the bullets of hate
in state, we lay on display
a small box contains the remains
sustains, jewels for viewing.

Fear is built into the human body
a negative emotion filled with the notion
incisions create deadly decisions
for those with licensed guns
to hunt for sport and fun
in the killing of unarmed black men.

Fall to the bullets of hate
in state, we lay on display
a small box contains the remains
sustains, jewels for viewing.

Fear makes them think

without a blink or wink
to sink their bullets
into bodies of black men.
Fear disguised, leads to the taking of lives
with a false sense of courage.

Fall to the bullets of hate
in state, we lay on display
a small box contains the remains
sustains, jewels for viewing.

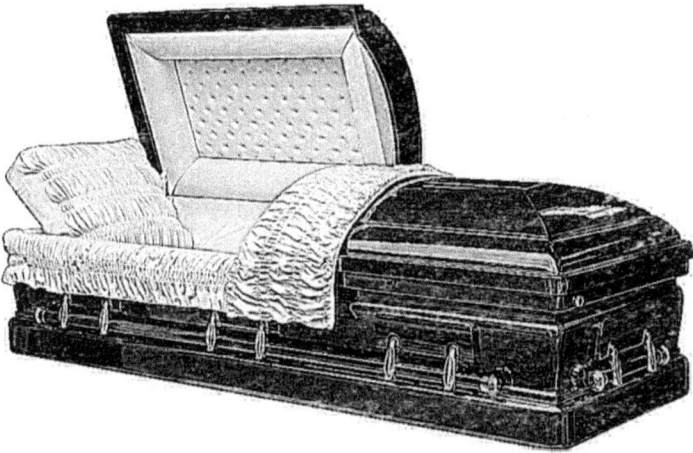

The Winds of Change

I too saw the raindrops fall from the trees
like morning dew on moist grass
withered leaves, wrinkled and fallen down
like hands in the air for Michael Brown.

Winds were strong
blowing, raging 'round
loud sound, emptying the house
filled the streets with marching people
black silence, deafening stillness
pain, hurt, anger, dead silence.

What my ears heard was a whispering.
A father/mother/God whose son lay bleeding
dying/mourning tender years of a baby's lullaby.

I told my soul
the sadness I felt
was coming from my human self.
Again, I felt the sadness
in the chambers of my heart
and told the people to:
"Pray in the songs of change
pray in the winds of change
pray in the seasons of change
pray in, and stay prayed up."

Time comes for new leaves to blow
caring, carving, craving, cradling
restoring healing, balance to the old meaning
of life's cycles once again.

Power Concedes Nothing without a Struggle

Men who speak in loud voices
claim, "I'm a grown-ass man."
without a bank account or a credit card.

Men who claim they are their own man
yet live between houses they don't even rent or own
men who claim they want a real woman
without having to put energy into a relationship.

They don't realize baby, they just don't realize
they... don't... realize
that the price of love is love,
and the price of greed is agony.

Men who claim they want a better life
yet continue to rob, steal, and kill
men who claim they want a change
yet they are not willing to be the change they want.

They don't realize baby, they just don't realize
they...don't...realize
that the price of love is love
and the price of greed is agony.

I say the limitations of oneself, locked in a cage
is defined by the willingness to endure injustices
perpetrated upon them.

When my people rise up, manipulation is over
when my people strive to thrive, exploitation is over
when my people stand up and speak
spark of the Divine Light shine in their eyes

teach my people to rise up, teach my people to thrive and strive
teach my people to organize, and be willing to stand to fight

because power concedes nothing without a struggle!
It never did and it never will.
Because the price of love is love
and the price of greed is agony.

Dem Streets Come Calling

I will keep you safe
I will kiss away your tears
I will give you plenty hugs

Dem streets come calling for you

I refuse to let you go
I refuse to let you go

I refused to turn you over
to the dope dealer
pusher man, number runner
po-po man, the feds, the jailers
institutions, or the undertakers

Dem streets come calling for you

I will not let them take you
from my breasts, from my womb
from your bed, from your home

Dem streets come calling for you

I refuse to let you go to the cello games
the crap games, dice games
the chain smokers, weed blowers
coke snorters, pants on the ground thugs

Dem streets come calling for you

I will cover you in my love
in my pavilion will I hide you
I will feather kiss you

my sweet chocolate son
erase your tears away

Dem streets come calling for you

Dem streets don't know how much
I love you

I will fight for you
I will hide you
I will forgive you
I will pray for you
I will nurture you
I will teach you
I must reach you
only as a mother can.

When dem streets come calling
I will stand—to answer
with a knock
knowing that we matter
built on the backs and the strength of our ancestors.

I Can't Breathe
(for Eric Garner)

As his voice cried out in a whisper
"I can't breathe... I can't breathe."

White man, cop, po-po,
"Why you bothering me, I ain't did nothing.
I just broke up a fight, leave me alone.
I ain't did nothing. Leave me alone."

As his voice cried out in a whisper
"I can't breathe... I can't breathe."

The autopsy showed Eric Garner
had no drugs or alcohol in his body.
It was the outlawed chokehold,
pinning him down to the ground
deadly pressure upon his throat
squeezed precious life from black man.

As his voice cried out in a whisper
"I can't breathe... I can't breathe."

His breathing became labored
signs of his short life
slowly, staggering, fading from glory
becoming that last possible sliver of light
before his final darkness.

As his voice cried out in a whisper
"I can't breathe... I can't breathe."

Choke hold forced upon his massive 350 pounds
strangles and cuts off air supply

homocide by white cop.

As his voice cried out in a whisper
for the last time: "I can't breathe... I can't breathe."

The Killing of Unarmed Michael Brown

Ferguson, you're kill'in me!
Ferguson, you're kill'in me!

Social unrest will be seen, felt and heard
until the you name the white cop
who murdered unarmed Michael Brown.

We shall shout, scream, march, loot, holler,
and disobey until the white walls of justice
gives ear to the rampant rage of race
and the killing of unarmed black men.

All police officers shall be held accountable
for the actions of failure to render aide,
and the murdering of an 18 year old teenager.

Does the massiveness of our black men fear you?
Do you shrink at the sight of black power
towering before you at 6'4 and 300 pounds?

Do the fearlessness of our black men
grab you with shame and fear
causing you to grip your gun tighter,
squeeze your trigger quicker,
refusing to release its grip
until all rounds in the chamber are spent?

Is inferiority and fear a conscious weapon
of choice against the Black Man?

The Killing of unarmed Michael Brown will not rest.
You may bring your rabid dogs and fire hoses of the 1960s
your bombs and tear gas of the 21st Century

but still you cannot defeat the black man,
you cannot kill the black man
for the essence of the black man
has been hidden from the white eyes of the world
through the power of his melanin
and will live on forever more...here and hereafter.

Note: Written before the naming of the White Police Office Darren Wilson

A Portrait of Sadness

A bruised heart
with broken wings
unable to take flight
in the white winds
of darkness.

A thin smile pretends
to cover his grief-stricken face
pain hidden beneath
his fabricated locks
to hide himself.

"I use locks to win the
affection of women,"
he confessed one day.

He used the growth of locks
to appear strong,
to appear stable
to appear aggressive
to sell weed
to the white tourists
and mimic Jamaican dialect.

Scars lyrically written upon his heart
he sings hoping for inner peace
he sings hoping for inner healing

with his sadness
he sings a song
full of the pain
that his short life has gain

he sings a song
black as a cloud
and black as his face
in a life that lies in waste.

He covers himself
before the final curtain
draped in a portrait of sadness.

He Does Not Beat Djembe Drums Anymore

He does not beat Djembe drums anymore
ancestors are too far removed from his heart
he does not beat Djembe drums anymore.

He tried to sell the Djembe drums
he tried to sell his ancestors blood
his fire has died
he does not beat Djembe drums anymore.

Lurking shadows
no stories will be told through Djembe drums
his fire has died.

He used to beat those Djembe drums
chant to his African Gods
walk black, talk black
and stood erect in his Black Power.

The island swallowed him up
and pitted him like a seed
unearthed in the ground
his fire has died.
He does not know how to beat Djembe drums anymore.

Brotha Man, Wake Up

Black Brotha, wake up!
You are not property for anyone to breed you.

You do not need to sleep with a non-black woman
in exchange for a place to rest your head.

No need to walk past your sistah
refusing to recognize or acknowledge her.

When you hold hands with the white woman,
your sistah does not care. That does not concern her.

What concerns your sistah is your refusal and your denial
'cause when you fail to see her
you deny yourself, as well as deny your very own mother
the woman who birthed you, as well as your aunts
and your daughter, and all the black women
unborn to you still yet. You deny a generation of black women.

The black woman who will always be your sistah
and will always represent or haunt you
as a painful shameful reminder of you taking the easier softer way.

Brotha wake up, and dream your own reality
and not the dream deferred!

Hostage or Husband

She mothered him in an unhealthy way
then weaned him from her competition
and bade him to her brown breasts
her only desire was to seek out
and penetrate his immeasurable gun
deep into her easy bake oven of whiteness.

Her father declared publicly that he was a deadbeat dad
who chased unsuccessfully after women
while cloaking his sexual frustrations and fraudulent
hypocrisy behind a Buddhist creed.

She, abandoned self, as surely father had abandoned her
flung caution to the wind to erase painful emotions
hidden in her bosom, he rested, unsure of himself, unsure of her
unto her bed she took him/he took her/and bore their monster
each a mirror for the other.

He about to feast on her, and she desperately closing in on him
locked in a torturous battle
both—running from self,
both—hiding—one from the other
cheating each other and one another.

Their mesh—between one another
holder and hostage taker
negotiator and traitor.

She didn't know what to expect
both struggled to move beyond the place of forgotten tears
until the final choice: the final cost
she knew he was one or the other
Hostage or Husband!

Black to Black

Brotha, your Mother
is your wise sage
the woman who fed you
bathed you and dressed you
when Father was absent

but only another black man
will rise up to support you
will raise you up to be whole, to be black
black to black brotha
the black man, Father and Mother got your back Brotha!

All that's Black Ain't Black

White people come in all colors
their racket consists of systems:
penal systems, institutional systems,
and judicial systems, social systems
cutting deep into the core
of our veins, red blood scarred back.

White face painted black
Ma Rainey black bottom
sings Billie Holiday 'strange fruit'
and that black boy standing
near you by the drinking fountain
is white.

How many times can you say
Uncle Tom Uncle Tom Uncle Tom
Uncle Tom Uncle Tom Uncle Tom?

Little Boy Lost
(For Tiger Woods)

The little boy is lost again
he doesn't know how to ski
but loves to play in snow
maybe because it is white
no, not the seven dwarfs
and snow white
black eludes him
little boy lost
tiger, when you fail to remember
you are doomed to repeat
Return home, Tiger
return home.

Section 10, Block F, Lot 12, Grave 4

Quiet solitude permeates the air
listening to the wind is the only sound I hear
nearby great trees stand tall
verdant oaks and elms stand tall
branches in air, whose arms are bare
like Michael Brown reaching for heaven.

In the frigid wind, I must discern my concern
I walk to section 10, block F, lot 12, and grave 4
no marker or headstone yet
plastic flowers mark the place and the spot
where Brown's parents cried from the depths of their soul
as they lowered his copper colored casket on the ground.

He stood a towering 6 feet 4, and then fell to the ground
when the white man emptied his gun into his body
his blackness shattered, stunned, his blood colored the dull
gray street.
He lay there for four hours
as the black folks experienced defeat in the street.

What a contrast there is between the first 18 years of life
and his final moment falling towards death on the asphalt
concrete.

Now I stand, in demand at his final resting place
where a white horse-drawn wagon delivered him
to the spot where the fresh flowers have died also.

It will be Thanksgiving soon, and we must look for gratitude
somewhere hidden in the clouds that gather
or new rains that cleanse the hearts of lost people.
And on its holiday heels, Christmas and Kwanzaa

will pay homage to this tragic year of 2014.

Our presents will be placed under the tree and the Zawadi
on the Kinara for Michael Brown and Ferguson, where
they will remain unopened until there is a rising up
and owning of hurtful actions, and admit errors,
egregious harms committed and ask for forgiveness
and show remorse in the taking of innocent lives.

Until we rid ourselves of a false fear and
unite in truth and true brotherhood,
only then will Ferguson be resolved with righteousness.

Michael Brown's exit from this world was cruel and swiftly executed.
What happens to the white policeman who killed him?
Why wait in fear and anxiety?
What decisions will the Grand Jury render?
Why wait for lies and the bone crushing juggernaut of hypocrisy to
set in?

I made a pilgrimage to his gravesite.
I stand here feeling the cold rattle my bones.
I leave the quiet solitude of St. Peter's Cemetery,
the storm of Ferguson and return to the melting pot
and double rainbows of Hawaii where Blacks make up
3.5% and know that Ferguson will be resolved in the here and now!

Note: This poem was written on November 24, 2014 two days before the Grand Jury's Decision.

Melvin

Red they called him
handsome as the sunrise in the east
shining his brilliant hues upon the ladies

I often looked up to Melvin.
He grew up and went into the Army.
I would follow him years later.

As an adult, he fell on hard times
and came to live with me.
I had gone to work one day as usual
and when I returned from work,
Melvin had sold my house to the drug dealers
who held me hostage in my home at gunpoint
for two nights, threatening to kill me if Melvin did not return.

How could the brother I loved do this to me?

I recalled how I much I adored my brother.
I enlisted in the United States Army like him.
As a child he was my chaperone who took me
to all my auditions, sat in the green room as I filmed
commercials and ran lines with fellow actors
from the television sitcom *Welcome Back Kotter*.

How could Melvin sell my home to drug dealers?

My home, my keys that held the answer to my life
my keys that represented freedom, and financial independence
my keys that produced more open doors in my young life.

How could Melvin sell my home to drug dealers?

What had I done to set up such an experience?

Years later, while l was living in Hawaii
Melvin's eldest son Michael who looks identical to Melvin
asked me, he asked me, me he asked, if he could come live with
me when he got paroled.
For one split nano second, I was about to tell him yes,
but then I realized that Michael was cut from his father's cloth
and I could not afford the thought of another home sold, while I
was at work.

Men like L. J. Yates

He stood a towering 6 ft 6"
tall, black, and handsome
his pretty green eyes and a complexion
reminiscent of the Arizona dessert
with red hues and pearly white teeth.
He was a lady's man
who had girlfriends of different races
and dated them all at the same time.

He walked around his whole life
with bow head to the white man
never feeling whole.
His life based on the legacy of slavery.
Oh how he could joke to the white man,
and make himself the brunt of his own
belittling black jokes
because he didn't know how to feel whole.

As a little girl of seven years,
she secretly peed in his shoes and cut up his shirts
an attempt to protect her mother from his abuse and
her own fear.

He took his anger out on his wife
but never his oppressor; the white man.
Eventually the distortion and the convolution
was bestowed upon his daughters and granddaughters;
his life based upon the legacy of slavery.

One day her mother asked her,
"I have forgiven him, why can't you?"

Little brown girl growing up in the deep racial divide.

She wanted her father to stand strong and not hide.
She wanted to see him as a towering peak
towards the white man. But the fact of the matter,
remains that he was weak, and she was able to see
his humiliation and his degradation in business life
his shame and blame, and his shadow-self.

She was able to see how defeated he felt in
the presence of the white man at that tender age.
She knew that his sub-conscious was strong
strong enough that he felt embarrassed on every level
based on his legacy of slavery.

On a deeper level, she knew his embarrassment
and rather than being embarrassed
based on his legacy of slavery
he pushed his beautiful doe eye daughter out of his life.

Because of his bowed head to the white man
socially and economically taught her
that she must always stand for something
or else she might fall to anything.

A lesson she learned to carry within her bosom
passed on to the delicate care of her five children
for seven decades.

She knew that in all his pain and ignorance
there is a human being, doing the best that
he knows how to do, in his state of consciousness.

She learned to remain in love and forgiveness
while healing her generational past!

FAITH AND TRUST

I Take Action in My Life

I have come full circle now
to realize that I need
to take action in my life.

If I focus on what I want
I am telling God
what my desires are.

I take action in my Life.

I am not afraid to step out
and make things happen
in my world.

I take action in my Life.

I know that when I leap
the net will appear
hard work and perseverance
makes me take action.

I take action in my Life now!

Not Everyone likes Black People

Not everyone will like black people
but it is okay to accept
then trying to make people like us
or people-please and be a phony
and not live an authentic life.

Times will come during life
when I will come across people
who do not like black people.

Like attracts like
so if they do not like black people
I remember that they are not like us,
they are not black people.

I claim my freedom
and leave others
to their own freedom.

I stay on my own path
depending upon God.

I follow my own inner guidance with integrity
I transcend limitations
and empower myself and my black people
to shine bright light and live sucker free.

Knowing

Looking within myself
I realize that answers are within me
and not without.
I seek life's questions
by going within.

No need do I ask others and look about.
I've always had the answers within.
Using my inner compass,
I trust, listen, embrace, love, listen
and act confidently with the direction
of one who knows.

I, too Sing Black America

I refuse to buy into the illusion of the world
I matter
my very existence
affects countless people in countless ways
the world simply could not exist
if black men were not it.

If you believe that your life
does not matter,
ask yourself, "Why you feel this way?"
make changes in your heart
and changes will be made in your life.

I share a sense of connection with the world.
I am black
I am male
I count
and I, too sing Black America.

Confrontation

He stepped out of the shower naked
having washed away the soot and blind confusion
he challenged himself in truth
between the lower realms of his darkness
and the higher halls of his consciousness

taking a good long look in the mirror
years of tears, mixed with fears, begin to escape
leaving a trail of broken hate, no longer to negate
his wait, and when he slowed the flow, long enough

authenticity emerged from the confines of his jail
in detail, revealed much more. What he saw shook his core.

Underneath the debris and phoniness, was the stark reality
that he was a boy, playing with his sister's dolls, pretending
to play house.

Only this time, he had aroused and married a wife
whom he didn't know, never bestow, his love, and a
child on the way, he say, he didn't want or need.

For in truth, he was that child, running wild, faking smiles
desperately needing to be loved, needing to be taken care of
and needing to be raised, again!

As he stood looking in the reflective mirror, for quite some time
years passed before him... standing in the mirror's raw reflection
of his boyhood...

He stepped back into the shower, gained power, and washed away
all that stood between him and manhood
all that stood between him and fatherhood

all that stood before him and claiming his masculinity...

and he exited the bath his final time, he would return to himself
embracing all that stood before his glorious Self
embracing a special kind of self-acceptance
embracing self-forgiveness
embracing a new course of life, without the possibility of failure.

And when he looked in the mirror again, he was finally able
to embrace all his shadow selves
to claim and to welcome with open arms
the small boy, the adult male, and grown man and come to know
that he is at the beginning of his magnificence, his strength,
his own awakening!

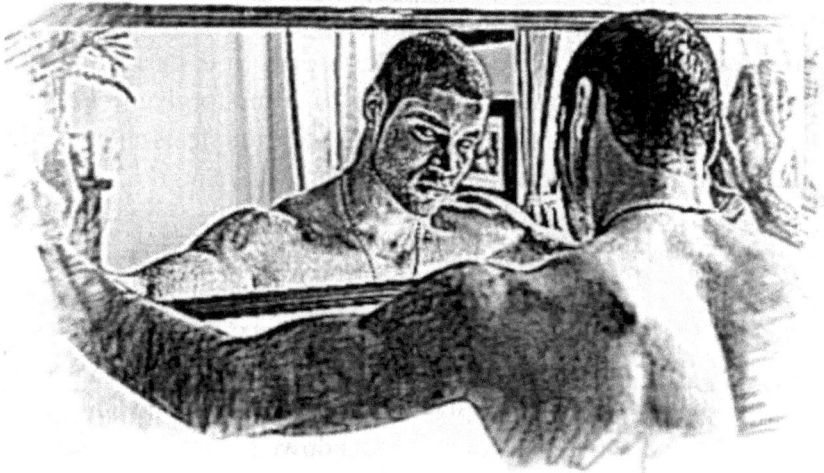

Dear Mother,

I want you to know that I see your grief and pain. I use to know pain and was very angry that my life was taken. He had no right to take my life. But now Mother, I am not concerned with setting things right, my focus is on seeing things rightly. I am now able to see from a higher awareness and with clarity. It was heavy for me on the planet to be weighed down with such heaviness as vengeance, violence, darkness, and grief. There is so much murkiness and denseness on earth.

All the experiences that are occurring on earth is occurring in man's reality, man's world, man's laws, man's punishments, man's justices, and has very little to do with love Mother. There is a spiritual law, which is unseen. Man has failed to utilize this gift. These laws set in motion Divine right action and work without seeing color, race, or creed. It is impermanent to those who use it.

I write this letter that bypasses your human senses, reaching deeply in your soul, to tell you that I understand forgiveness clearly. I know love Mother. You may call upon me for help, protection, and support. In my light of understanding and peace, forgiveness and oneness, I represent a wellspring from which you can lovingly draw strength and wisdom in times of need on the earth plane. It comes from Oneness.

I understand that you and countless other mothers are experiencing what may seem to be a lifetime of injustices and tribulations. Please know that these too, are a part of human existence. Do not become distracted by the loud noise that echoes around you. I ask you to go within. I urge you to ground yourself in love and forgiveness, using wisdom and understanding. I will help you with your fears and feelings of helplessness and insecurities, worries and anxieties.

I see the people on earth in grief, pain, and their temptations for violence and revenge. I see their unwavering marches and cries of more marches and rallies. I see no one comforting the people. Please know that I bring you comfort. Feel my presence mother, and know that I am with you always. Feel me breathe a cool peace upon your soul. You will come to know that together we will fulfill what needs to be done, for we have always been endowed from the beginning of mankind. We are resilient and extremely well fitted and equipped. Mother, when you choose to know, you will remember how we are connected to a greater power, stronger than any man of color, more prosperous than earthly finances and possessions. We are of a rare purity that is often punished, frowned upon, and inhumanly seized upon in a negative degrading way. All will be revealed in due time.

I want you to know that my entire journey on earth was monitored, because I needed to do my best, and I have completed my journey.

Mother, I speak directly to you in your dreams, in your prayers, and in the face of other men. Please know that we have made contact. Realize that deep down in your soul, we have reached one another.

I want to thank you for giving me the gift of life. I honor your life as mother, as a black woman, and as a feeling thinking praying woman. Thank you for being part of the sacred web of life. Now that you know these truths, you must go forth in love and compassion as you continue to evolve as a spiritual being who is growing through the human experience.

Know that I love you always Mother and that I forgive everyone and I ask you to forgive them too, for they know not what they do. I am free. I love you.

Until Soon,
Your Son,

Sean Bell, Amadou Diallo, Rodney King, Trayvon Martin, Michael Brown, Eric Garner, Tamir Rice and others whose seat that I keep warm as their light which burns bright, make their way home.

Walking Down Life's Road

He told me that he was walking down life's road one dark and lonely night. He was one block away from home. He was tired, cold and hungry, discontented and sick, and wanted to get home to eat his chicken noodle soup, and drink a cup of hot tea. He could feel his consciousness leaving him as he fell to the ground, spilling his groceries from his arms.

Regaining composure, he stared down the barrel of a shotgun and a loud voice bellowing, "Nigger get up, and get off my damn property." As he tried to stand up, he was keeping an eye on the white man's trigger finger and his other eye on the muzzle of the shotgun that followed him, brushing against his cheek ever so slightly.

"I'm warning you nigger, get off my damn property," the white man said. Bending down again, he began to retrieve the spilled contents from his pack, slowly picking up his food, a calming peace washed over him deeply and profoundly. He sank back down to his knees, unable to move. Blackness came to claim him.

Using his shotgun as a stick, touching my nose, the white man said, "Hey nigger boy, hey boy wake up, wake up." Fading in and out of consciousness, I vaguely said, "Help me brother." Slowing coming to, I no longer felt lonely or in fear for my life. I felt serenity moving upon me like dolphins on water and a trusting peace enveloped me. I allowed this new power to mingle with my power as I slowly took it all in. It was overwhelming.

It seemed like I was fully awake when what the man did next. There was a powerful presence diffusing a negative situation and entering the realms of a new and higher calling, a higher divinity. The energy had begun to circle us and it seemed like a third being hovered above us. Next, I witnessed the energy circling the white man's shotgun as if to remove it from his hand. The shot gun dropped to the ground as the man reached for his hose and turned the water on full blast, then he aimed the hose me. The water stirred me.

I came to again, and in that moment there was something so mysterious and calming that had permeated the space. I sat up praying and thanking the God of my own understanding.

Something had come over him. He looked down at his gun, he looked up to the sky, and then he asked me if I were okay. I remained humble and full of faith. Next, he held my head as I continued drinking water from the hose he held. Again, it felt like there were three of us present; me, him, and the presence!

He began to ask me where I lived and about my fainting episode. He listened intently as I told him about myself, and how down I was feeling tonight. He helped me to my feet.

As we picked up my groceries from the ground, I told him that I lived around the corner. And that I was born in the house that my grandparents had built. I told him about my family easily and effortlessly. He met me with the same assurance and with his own grace. He was telling me about his family and how his father and grandfather was a racist and a bigot. He told me how they did mean things to black people and were expecting him to follow in their footsteps.

His father and grandfather had drilled it in him and prepared him to be ready. He told me that he was ready to kill him one tonight, until I fainted and called him brother and a certain immeasurable grace had befallen him.

I listened carefully, remaining receptive and open to his heart, and I knew that in that moment, there was a power and a presence and a purpose that had brought us together.

Before long, we were standing in front of my home. He smiled at my home, and then smiled at me. I thanked him for walking me home and for saving my life, instead of taking it. We both felt it and saw it that night.

I was open and receptive to seeing physically, mentally, spiritually, and emotionally what others have been taught to believe and to live. I also saw that with no experience of their own, they would fall prey to victimizing others. As I walked down life's dark road that night, life lit up my soul and I've never been the same since.

About the Author

Ayin M. Adams, PhD. Msc.D., is a native New Yorker. She is also an international metaphysician, spiritual director, and intuitive therapist. Adams is a holistic teacher of self-development and consciousness. Adams utilizes her gift of words to heal, educate, and entertain.

Adams is the author of more than eight books. Adams has been published by "Women in the Moon" publishing, *Bum Rush The Page*, *In The Family*, and *Quiet Mountain Essays*. Adams is the 2015 Beverly Hills Book Awards Finalist for her book, *African Americans in Hawai`i: A Search for Identity*, the 2015 *Bronze Medal Illumination Book Award* winner, 1998 winner of the *Pat Parker Poetry Award*, the 1999 *Audre Lorde Memorial Prose Prize*, the 2001 *President's Award for Literary Excellence*, and the *Zora Neal Hurston/Richard Wright Award*. Adams documents our passage in time using her writings and tonality of voice to help one break out of the current constraints and fragmentation of daily and habitual life. She assists

and facilitates individuals to co-create their futures, especially as many of the established structures of society may be falling apart. Adams lives with the intention of suiting up, showing up, and following through. Adams embraces a firm belief that everything is in Divine Order. Ayin M. Adams organizes and leads spiritual retreats geared towards the transformational transcendence of mind, body, and soul. She makes her home in Maui. You may visit her at www.ayinadams.com.

www.ingramcontent.com/pod-product-compliance
Lightning Source LLC
Chambersburg PA
CBHW060542100426
42742CB00013B/2424